SBB

SWASTICK BOOK BOX

MASON OF WINNERS

Cursive

WORD WRITING

Workbook - 4

Awesome Cursive Writing Practice Book for Kids

By: **Preeti Garg**

Follow the patterns with your pencil.

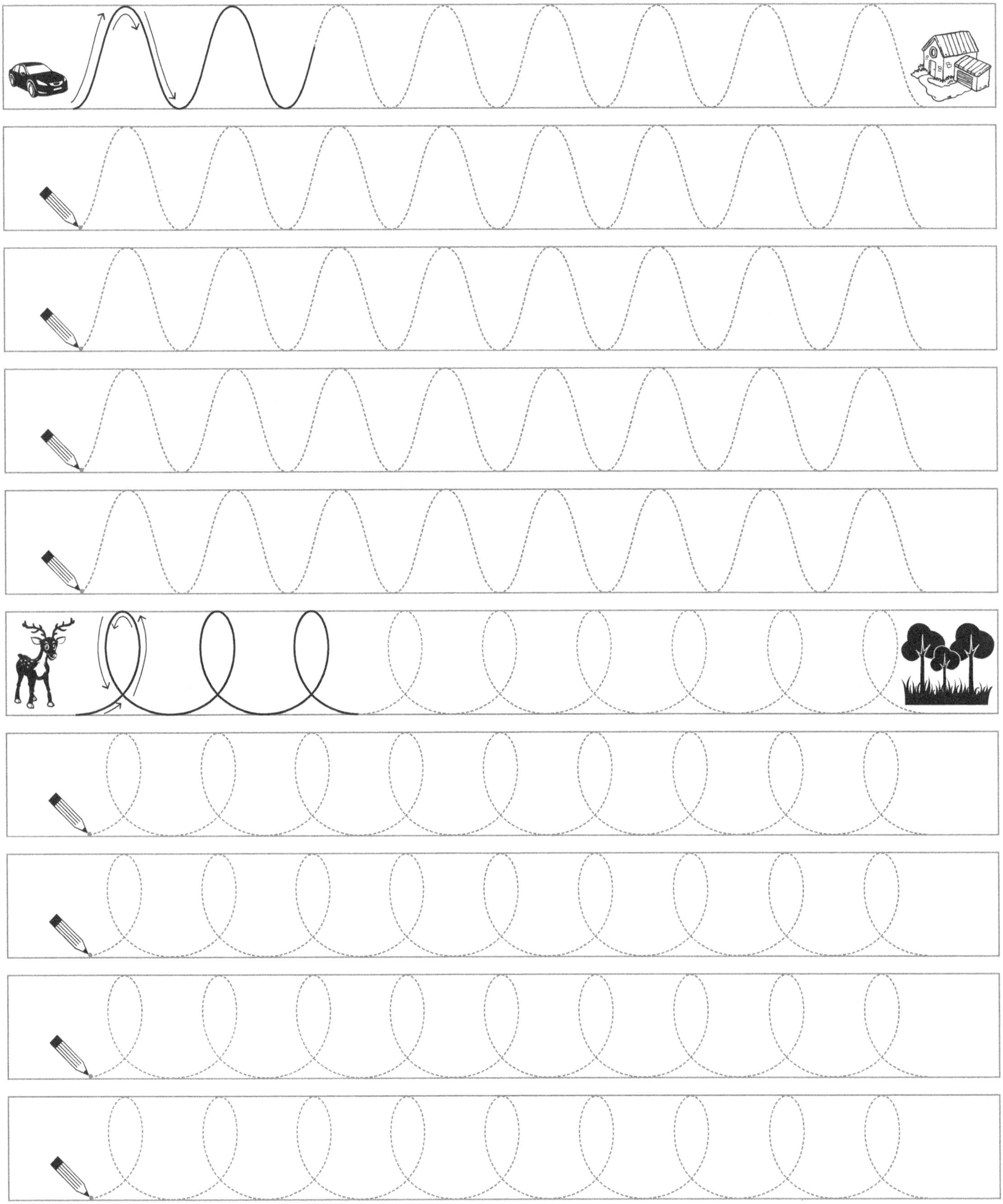

Say and trace the letters.

Ab	Bc	Cd	De	Ef
ab	bc	cd	de	ef
Fg	Gh	Hi	Ij	Jk
fg	gh	hi	ij	jk
Kl	Lm	Mn	No	Op
kl	lm	mn	no	op
Pq	Qr	Rs	St	Tu
pq	qr	rs	st	tu
Uv	Vw	Wx	Xy	Yz
uv	vw	wx	xy	yz

Say and trace the letters.

Abc	Bcd	Cde	Def	Efg
abc	bcd	cde	def	efg
Fgh	Ghi	Hij	Ijk	Jkl
fgh	ghi	hij	ijk	jkl
Klm	Lmn	Mno	Nop	Opq
klm	lmn	mno	nop	opq
Pqr	Qrs	Rst	Stu	Tuv
pqr	qrs	rst	stu	tuv
Uvw	Vwx	Wxy	Xyz	
uvw	vwx	wxy	xyz	

Date : ....

Teacher's Signature : ....

Say and trace the letters.

Abcd	Bcde	Cdef	Defg	Efgh
abcd	bcde	cdef	defg	efgh
Fghi	Ghij	Hijk	Ijkl	Jklm
fghi	ghij	hijk	ijkl	jklm
Klmn	Lmno	Mnop	Nopq	Opqr
klmn	lmno	mnop	nopq	opqr
Pqrs	Qrst	Rstu	Stuv	Tuvw
pqrs	qrst	rstu	stuv	tuvw
Uvwx	Vwxy	Wxyz		
uvwx	vwxy	wxyz		

Date : ....

Teacher's Signature : ....

Elephant  Buffalo  Kangaroo 

Elephant	Buffalo	Kangaroo
Elephant	Buffalo	Kangaroo
elephant	buffalo	kangaroo
elephant	buffalo	kangaroo

Sunflower  Tulips  Hibiscus 

Sunflower	Tulips	Hibiscus
Sunflower	Tulips	Hibiscus
sunflower	tulips	hibiscus
sunflower	tulips	hibiscus

Pumpkin  Zucchini  Capsicum 

Pumpkin	Zucchini	Capsicum
Pumpkin	Zucchini	Capsicum
pumpkin	zucchini	capsicum
pumpkin	zucchini	capsicum

Date : .... Teacher's Signature : ....

Raspberry  Nectarine  Avocado 

Raspberry	Nectarine	Avocado
Raspberry	Nectarine	Avocado
raspberry	nectarine	avocado
raspberry	nectarine	avocado

Fisherman  **Mechanic**  **Watchman** 

Fisherman	Mechanic	Watchman
Fisherman	Mechanic	Watchman
fisherman	mechanic	watchman
fisherman	mechanic	watchman

Monday	Tuesday	Wednesday
Monday	Tuesday	Wednesday
Thursday	Friday	Saturday
Thursday	Friday	Saturday
Sunday		
Sunday		

January	February	March
January	February	March
April	May	June
April	May	June

Date : ....

Teacher's Signature : ....

July	August	September
July	August	September
October	November	December
October	November	December

Yesterday	Today	Tomorrow
Yesterday	Today	Tomorrow
Morning	Afternoon	Evening
Morning	Afternoon	Evening
Night	Tonight	Fortnight
Night	Tonight	Fortnight

Spring	Autumn	Summer
Spring	Autumn	Summer
Winter	Year	Leapyear
Winter	Year	Leapyear
Decade	Century	Millennium
Decade	Century	Millennium

No one is perfect.

No one is perfect.

Being kind is never wasted.

Being kind is never wasted.

A bad tax needs an axe.

A bad tax needs an axe.

Eat a healthy diet.

Eat a healthy diet.

Live the golden rule.

Live the golden rule.

Strive for excellence!

Strive for excellence!

Go to school on time.

Go to school on time.

Comb your hair daily.

Comb your hair daily.

Respect your teachers.

Respect your teachers.

Always tell the truth.

Always tell the truth.

Practice good hygiene.

Practice good hygiene.

Brush your teeth twice.

Brush your teeth twice.

Be a voice, not an echo.

Be a voice, not an echo.

Always do what is right.

Always do what is right.

We grow great by dreams.

We grow great by dreams.

Find a small win each day.

Find a small win each day.

Life is a daring adventure.

Life is a daring adventure.

Drink a lot of pure water.

Drink a lot of pure water.

Cross road at zebra crossing.

Cross road at zebra crossing.

Develop good study habits.

Develop good study habits.

Life is short spend it happy.

Life is short spend it happy.

Familiarity breeds contempt.

Familiarity breeds contempt.

Own not the most but the best.

Own not the most but the best.

Die with memories not dreams.

Die with memories not dreams.

Date : ....

Teacher's Signature : ....

little things make big days.

little things make big days.

Smiling increases your face value.

Smiling increases your face value.

Small aim is crime; have great aim.

Small aim is crime; have great aim.

Flowers, flowers everywhere,

In the garden, in my hair.

In the vase and at the store.

On the table, on the door.

What a lovely time of year.

Flowers blooming, bringing cheer.

Date : ....

Teacher's Signature : ....

A little seed for me to sow,

A little soil to make it grow.

A little hole, a little pat,

A little wish, and that is that.

A little sun, a little shower,

A little while, and a flower.

Twinkle, Twinkle, little star.

How I wonder what you are.

Up above the world so high,

Like a diamond in the sky.

Twinkle, Twinkle, little star.

How I wonder what you are.

Red as a sunset,

Orange as a juice.

Yellow as a baby chick,

Green as a bunch of grapes.

Blue as an ocean,

Purple as a juicy plum.

Date : ....

Teacher's Signature : ....

Doctors save lives.

Doctors give medicine.

Doctors are friendly.

Doctors work in hospital.

Doctors save lives.

Doctors give medicine.

Doctors are friendly.

Doctors work in hospital.

I love my mother.

My mother teaches me.

My mother is a homemaker.

My mother loves me a lot.

I love my mother.

My mother teaches me.

My mother is a homemaker.

My mother loves me a lot.

Date : ....

Teacher's Signature : ....

This is a dog.

Dog is a pet animal.

Dogs are of many kinds.

The dog is a faithful animal.

This is a dog.

Dog is a pet animal.

Dogs are of many kinds.

The dog is a faithful animal.

Date : ....

Teacher's Signature : ....

Mango is a fruit.

Mango is very juicy.

Mango is the national fruit.

Mango is the king of fruits.

Mango is a fruit.

Mango is very juicy.

Mango is the national fruit.

Mango is the king of fruits.